A LETTER IN YOUR LOSS

Living Through The Sorrow Of Miscarriage

KRISTEN KELLEY

The Guild of Baptist Writers

For Joshua and Finlay
Absent from the body - Present with the Lord

CONTENTS

FOREWORD

A Letter in Your Loss are words from Kristen Kelley's heart and soul.

Kristen is a young mother who suffered two miscarriages.

In this book, Kristen shares the hope and comfort she found in Christ during her seasons of grief.

A Letter in Your Loss uses Scripture, portions of hymns, and excerpts from the author's own blog and diary.

This book is a letter of empathy and encouragement to ladies walking through a similar sorrow.

PREFACE

A Letter in Your Loss notes citations with this formatting:

Scripture Citations look like this:

"*Who comforteth us in all our tribulation, that we may be able to comfort them which are in any trouble, by the comfort wherewith we ourselves are comforted of God.*" (2 Corinthians 1:4)

Hymn Citations look like this:

> "*Thou changest not,*
> *Thy compassions,*
> *they fail not . . .*
> *Great is Thy faithfulness.*"

Blog or Diary Quotations:

FROM MY BLOG:

FROM MY DIARY:

INTRODUCTION

Dear Aching One,

Where do I even begin? You lost your baby . . . A part of your life is gone forever. . .

You hold this letter in your hand because your face is tear-stained, and your womb is now empty. . .

Perhaps you do not want to hear from me. More than likely, you do not even know me.

I am probably a complete stranger to you . . . But I am a stranger who understands how deeply your heart is hurting, and how painful it is to have shattered hopes and dreams.

Sometimes it helps just to know that someone else has been where you sit, right now. And when you are ready - when you are ready to reach out for a glimmer of hope and light in your darkness - I pray you will allow me to hug you across these pages.

If you are in need of a friend, I am here for you. If you need comfort, I know the Someone Who can mend the broken pieces . . .

"Who comforteth us in all our tribulation, that we may be able to comfort them which are in any trouble, by the comfort wherewith we ourselves are comforted of God."

— II CORINTHIANS 1:4

SAYING GOODBYE

My New Friend,

In December of 2016, we were weeping, too.

At 21 weeks pregnancy, we had taken our four girls with us into an ultrasound room, anxious to see a healthy, kicking Baby #5. We planned a fun gender reveal party for Christmas Day - we were even going to Skype it for my parents, living hundreds of miles away.

You know what we saw on the screen instead . . . You know that painful silence instead of a heartbeat . . . You know . . . And we turned to the confused faces of our beautiful little girls, and through our tears, we told them that the baby in Mommy's tummy had gone to be with Jesus.

The instructions and the options that followed were such a blur. In the end, we decided to be induced into labor and to deliver our baby in the hospital. I want to share with you something that I wrote on my blog, from the depths of my heart, shortly after we said that final "goodbye" to our precious Joshua. I want you to know the comfort God brought me from His Word during some of the darkest days of my life. I pray you will be able to bring yourself to read it – even if the tears flow down your cheeks, as they still do my own:

> *There is so much about this type of grief that can't be shared, but my heart longs to write - has always needed to write - during the emotional moments of my life. What I CAN tell you is that the delivery was long, and difficult, and tearful. I can tell you that my husband was wonderful, and went through every step of this tragic journey with me. I can tell you that people were praying for our family on every corner of the globe, and that we felt God's Presence, His grace, and His strength in a way we had never known before.*

> *This past Wednesday night, I stayed at home and rested in anticipation of labor the following day. I'll never forget how in the quiet peacefulness of those hours alone, I was able to listen to instrumental music and stitch a little blanket outfit to put on our baby. The photo of it makes my heart smile. It was what I dressed him in when we said our sweet goodbyes. Only God can make such moments beautiful.*

> *On Friday morning, December 16th, 2016, our little boy, Joshua David Kelley, was delivered. He was very small – his face not quite as fully developed as we had imagined – but his tiny legs, and knees, and feet, his arms and his*

hands, were precious. Mommy kissed his feet
several times before she told him "goodbye" . . . I
kiss our Charlotte's now and think about those
sad kisses every time. How VERY grateful we
were to God that we had our sweet girls at
home! Whenever they hug us or rub our backs,
it heals us. Whenever they smile or giggle a
contagious giggle, it heals us. Whenever they
ask a child's question about the loss of our baby,
or about Heaven, it comforts our hearts to
answer them.

A local church donates blankets to Sentara RMH
for deliveries such as ours, and we received a
purple one. It is a treasured gift that, for now,
still smells like the hospital. The familiar odor
and sounds of that floor made me weep when
we first walked up to the registration desk, but
now the lingering scent brings me comfort. I've
been sleeping with that purple blanket lately . .
. maybe to somehow help the Mommy heart
that would have been snuggling a newborn . . .
And we have the most precious "Forever In
Our Hearts" wind chimes hanging in the
kitchen – a present that friends in college sent to
us after they learned of our sad news. Joshua
never made a sound, but those wind chimes do,
and it, too, heals Mommy's heart.

On Sunday, I craved the blessing of sitting in
church and hearing the Christmas hymns being
sung. Despite the physical pain, I was so
thankful to be there as a family, even for just
the morning service. The girls wore their

3

Christmas dresses – Jacqueline's was a sparkly present from Grammy & Grampa – and Charlotte got to ride in her new front-facing car seat for the first time. She must have felt like she was on the rocket ship from the "Little Einstein" shows because she automatically began saying "pat-pat-pat-pat" for the take-off. Even amid our grief, there are moments when we can smile and laugh. Only God can do that, Dear Friends! I pray that none of you ever have to go through such a horribly dark tragedy as we walked through, this past week, but if you do, GOD IS THERE! And you have no idea how beautiful those valleys can be when He is by your side!

From the precious farewells, to all our memory-making for Little Joshua, to the daily family moments with our girls – God has been in ALL of it. Despite the tears, we find that we can even anticipate a special Christmas, together. How we thank and praise the Lord for such unforgettable days! He is our Rock and our Fortress, and He is GOOD! Please always know that, Friends! We have been walking through the "valley of the shadow of death," and God is here! My husband and I are going through this valley together, and are becoming more in love with each other than ever before. There is no anger in our grief – Our God is trustworthy! And oh, how He sweetly sends His comfort our way! People from church have brought us meals and washed our dishes; they even offered to help us

*wrap our Christmas presents . . . I will never,
ever forget this December . . . And that is
why I desired so to write to you all and
to share.*

*Psalm 145:2 declares, "Every day will I bless thee;
and I will praise thy name for ever and ever."
Every day . . . Not just the good ones . . . Even
on the day your body refuses over and over
again to accept the sorrowful fact that you are
being forced to go into labor . . . Even on the
day you hold a very tiny, lifeless body in your
hands, and say "goodbye" . . . Even on the day
you come home from the hospital with no little
newborn to cradle and kiss . . . EVERY day . . .
Psalm 55:17 "Evening, and morning, and at
noon, will I pray, and cry aloud: and he shall
hear my voice." No matter when the tears
come, God is there. He loves me so much that he
even keeps every tear in a bottle (Psalm 56:8). "
. . . yea, in the shadow of thy wings will I make
my refuge, until these calamities be overpast."
(Psalm 57:1) "He is the "God of all comfort."
(II Corinthians 1:3)*

*Do you know my Sweet Savior? Have you trusted
Him to save your soul? Romans 5:8 says, "But
God commendeth his love toward us, in that,
while we were yet sinners, Christ died for us."
He stretched out His arms when He died on the
cross for your sins and mine, and His arms are
still open for you to run into today. Romans
10:9 promises, "That if thou shalt confess with
thy mouth the Lord Jesus, and shalt believe in*

*thine heart that God hath raised him from the
dead, thou shalt be saved."*

*This peace that we know in our trial and our
tragedy? That isn't something you can find in a
prescription, or in a counseling book, or even in
the sweet reassurance of a friend. Our peace
comes from GOD, and YOU can know His
peace as well! His salvation "full and free" is
available to ANYONE who calls upon Him
in sweet, childlike faith. I pray that if you
know Him not, that you will trust in Jesus
Christ today!*

*Do you know why this Christmas Season can still
be bright in our sorrow? Because I have not
"lost" our Baby Boy . . . This Mommy knows
exactly where to find him. We shall see you
again, Little One – because Heaven is
our home.*

I will never forget those raw emotions, nor the bleak
color of the sky, nor the fierce coldness of the air. Those are
things forever embedded in my mind. And you have your
memories. These days of grief are a time in your life, that,
as a woman and a mother, you never forget. But, I pray you
look back one day on a healing comfort too — a solace you
found that only a loving Savior could give . . .

❧ 2 ❧

A SECOND LESSON IN SORROW

PERHAPS YOU HAVE BEEN HERE MORE THAN ONCE . . . MY heart hears yours too, Dear One. I do not know the gender of the baby from our second loss. In December of 2017, we were not as far along in our pregnancy as we had been with Joshua. But it brought me much joy to give that second Little One a name, and to know that he or she was safely in Heaven with our Lord. Precious Finlay was a baby whom I carried for 11 weeks . . . A baby whom I prayed so hard would be our "rainbow" . . . But it was not meant to be. I pray that as you read the verses and the peaceful thoughts that God gave me in our second grief, your own heart might be comforted too!

FROM MY BLOG:

> *Psalm 63:6 "When I remember thee upon my bed,*
> *and meditate on thee in the night watches."*
> *I didn't want to look at another lifeless ultrasound*
> *ever again . . . But sometimes what we dread*

the very most ends up coming to pass . . . Only those who have walked this road can truly understand. You feel like you've plunged beneath a frozen, icy pond, and you're gasping for breath. You hear the voices of your other children playing, but you can hardly pull yourself from the bed . . . It is the weight and cloud of grief . . . You're not taking fun family photos, or planning goals for the new year, like all the world seems to be, around you. You're just trying to live through TODAY . . . Trying not to be in physical pain . . . Trying to hold back the tears every time an article of clothing makes you remember what was finally a noticeable "bump," only a couple of weeks ago.

Any death can be tragic; saddening; devastating – but a miscarriage leaves a woman feeling HOLLOW as no other grief in the world can do - especially if you are a Christian mother. Because of your belief in God's Word, you understand how REAL it all is, right from the very beginning. Life was growing within you, a heart was beating close to your own - and then it was gone . . . Studies in recent years have shown that when we have carried babies in our womb, their cells sometimes even leave imprints on our own, changing us forever. Once you become a mom, you're truly never the same. Once you have miscarried, you're never the same, either. Such loss molds your heart in an entirely new way – a deeper way than ever before.

They tell you that you feel grief because you have felt LOVE. Oh how true that is! You may be wondering, "How can your heart hurt so much over a fifth baby or a sixth?" It aches because I have enjoyed the "baby stage" of motherhood so very, very much! I have embraced it as a gift from God. And I truly long for another wobbly little head on my shoulder at midnight. Perhaps you'd say with the well-meaning, "You already have four beautiful children . . ." But a mother's love does not get divided amongst her children; it only multiplies! And so, yes, a loving mother does grieve – whether it be the loss of her first or her tenth child.

Often in these sorrows, there are no answers. Once again, everything appeared to be "going just fine." So what do you do when there seems to be no "why"? As the beautiful church song goes,

> *"And there seems to be no reason for the suffering we feel;*
> *We are tempted to believe God does not know . . .*
> *And when you don't understand the purpose of His plan,*
> *in the Presence of the King, bow the knee."*

ANYONE we love here on earth is only a gift for a time. Some are with us for 11 weeks, but never held in our arms; others are by our side for 50 years or more. We ought to love them as God would have us love them – every single

day. But we ought to love Our Savior
even more.

> "All to Jesus I surrender,
> All to Him I freely give;
> I will ever love and trust Him,
> In His Presence daily live . . ."

One baby . . . Two babies . . . And any more of those
dearest in all the world to me that God chooses
to call home. They are Thine, O Lord!

And then, when we sorrow, we " . . . sorrow not,
even as others which have no hope." (I Thess.
4:13) Much in my heart has been crushed, and
there have been many, many tears. But our
2017 baby was taken to a glorious Heaven, by a
good and loving God. And I will see both my
miscarried babies in Heaven someday!

As my husband and I sat together in the hospital
room, I wrote these words from my heart:

"Heaven is on my mind today. The sweetest nursery
you could ever hope to see . . . Every baby
loved, and wished for, but never held on earth .
. . Every baby left, neglected, now cared for by
the angels . . . Every baby aborted in the womb,
but now 'loved on' by millions of mamas in a
perfect land . . . Every baby who suffered from
illnesses and birth defects, here below, now and
forever healed . . . Perhaps there are volunteers
who work 'nursery' in that Heavenly Place - If
so, I will certainly be one of them."

Hebrews 11:1 "Now faith is the substance of things hoped for, the evidence of things not seen."

With My Lord's help, through the sorrow and the pain, I choose to hold on to FAITH. Faith that God is good. Faith that " . . . his tender mercies are over all his works." (Psalm 145:9) Faith that He will heal the brokenness once again. Faith that no matter how many times I "go down to the grave," my Lord will bring me up (Psalm 30:3). Faith that joy will come in the morning (Psalm 30:5).

The words of the timeless hymn sound in my heart,

> *"Thou changest not,*
> *Thy compassions,*
> *they fail not . . .*
> *Great is Thy faithfulness."*

I do not know your name, or where you live. I do not know if you have a husband or a child at home to hug in your grief, or if you are feeling all alone in the world right now. But through these first few pages, you caught a glimpse of my own heart. You heard both of my personal stories of heartache and loss. I know how much a miscarriage can devastate and hurt. But I also know that My Loving Heavenly Father is truly *the God of all comfort* (II Cor. 1:3), even in the deepest of sorrows. He will walk alongside you, as no one in all the world can do.

꙳ 3 ꙳

FINDING PEACE IN YOUR PAIN

YOU ARE READING THIS LETTER BECAUSE YOU JUST miscarried at home . . . You endured a hospital delivery, or a surgical procedure called a D & E or a D & C . . . Maybe you just stood beside the smallest casket you have ever seen . . . You are a mom, and you are in need of peace as you wonder, "Where has my baby gone?"

One of the hardest decisions I ever had to make was what to do with the precious little body of our son. You have been there too. You know the questions. You recall the painful mental images you have to keep pushing from your mind . . . But is that the end – the awful decision of what happens with your sweet baby's remains? No, Friend, it is not the end. The Bible tells us that there is life after death – even for those we never hold in our hands.

Psalm 139 beautifully describes to us how God weaves and orchestrates everything that happens in the womb. He is in charge of every single detail. Before we know the eye color or the hair color, our baby's features are already written in His book (139:16). Jeremiah 1:5 declares, "*Before I formed thee in the belly I knew thee; and before thou camest forth*

out of the womb I sanctified thee . . ." God allowed you to carry
life – for no matter how brief or lengthy a period of time.
Even though it is painfully difficult trying to comprehend a
loving God allowing a baby to go straight from the womb
to Heaven's shores, we can sing with the hymn writer:

> *"Oh, yes, He cares,*
> *I know He cares,*
> *His heart is touched with my grief . . ."*

No matter what transpires in my life, I can trust that
God knows best! I cling to the knowledge that God is
GOOD! *"I had fainted, unless I had believed to see the goodness of
the LORD in the land of the living."* (Psalm 27:13)

Is there anger behind your tears? Hebrews 12:15 speaks
of a *"root of bitterness."* When going through difficulties and
trials in this life, it is easy to feed one's mind the sort of
bitter, poisonous thoughts that steal our peace and devour
our joy. "Why was HER baby allowed to live?" . . . "We
would have given ours a far better home than they will ever
give theirs" . . . "Why should she have so many children and
we cannot even have one?". . . "We are living for God! Why
must we go through this?" . . . Or perhaps you are tempted
to point blame – on the doctor, the hospital, the midwife,
the medical equipment . . . When the poisons of Satan start
to feed your mind, you must pray them away, Dear One!
Such thoughts and feelings will not heal your broken heart
– they will keep you shattered and will hurt those closest to
you. The Bible warns us *"Neither give place to the devil."*
(Ephesians 4:27) Refuse to allow even a little ROOT of
bitterness to take hold in your soul!

But what do you do, when all you can think about is the
child that was "taken away"? Our children belong to God
from the moment of their conception. He is their Creator.

He gives them heartbeat and breath . . . and He chooses when to call them Home. He knows ALL our appointments with life and with death. But so often, we do not understand. We want to hold on tightly to those we love. We want to feel in control. I urge you to surrender to Our Sovereign God, Dear Hurting One . . . *"In whose hand is the soul of every living thing, and the breath of all mankind."* (Job 12:10) Let Him be in control - trust Him, even when it is hardest to do so – and allow Him to comfort your heart. *"And we know that all things work together for good to them that love God, to them who are the called according to his purpose."* (Romans 8:28)

The day will come when your once-stretched tummy will go back down to size, and the maternity clothes will have to be put away. There might even be a bassinet, or a stack of onesies, purchased in love, that you know can not stay out forever. How does one "pack up" their hopes and their dreams? By giving them to the Master. That is the only way I know how: by letting Him be the "Keeper of the Dreams" – trusting Him with every today and all your tomorrows. *"Jesus Christ the same yesterday, and to day, and for ever."* (Hebrews 13:8)

Amid your tears, surround yourself with the things of God – His Word, His people, His creation. I encourage you to listen to peaceful hymns, watch golden sunsets, or dig deep in the soil of your flower garden. Live life, even when you feel there is no life left to live. There IS life in Christ! Has He given you breath? Has He saved your soul? Has He surrounded you with people who love you? Make that "thankfulness list" long, and cry sweet tears over God's blessings. Oh! In your darkest hour, God is GOOD!

But what about Heaven? How can I truly know that my child is there? II Samuel 12 tells the story of a sorrowing King David, praying that God will spare his infant son.

When he hears the news that the baby has died, he tells his servants, "*I shall go to him, but he shall not return to me.*" (12:23) Your baby cannot come back to you, but he or she is not gone forever! Your child is safe in Heaven, where there is no more crying, no more darkness, no more pain . . . (Rev. 21+22). If Heaven is your own eternal home, then you will have a sweet reunion one day! But do you have that assurance in your heart?

Perhaps you read the ending of my story about our Joshua, and you are wondering about "trusting in Jesus." God knows the sorrow of losing a child. He gave His only Son to die on the cross FOR US! "*For God so loved the world, that he gave his only begotten Son, that whosoever believeth in him should not perish, but have everlasting life.*" (John 3:16) Jesus was sinless – perfect. He paid the penalty for every sin we have ever committed or ever will commit. When we place our faith in His perfect payment for our wrongdoing, we receive new life in Christ. "*Therefore if any man be in Christ, he is a new creature: old things are passed away; behold, all things are become new.*" (II Corinthians 5:17) Before that cleansing of your heart, there is no peace. After you become His child, God grants you peace that "*passeth all understanding*" (Philippians 4:7) – a deeper peace than you can even comprehend. And, in that overwhelming calm, you gain the strengthening knowledge that His love is real, that He has prepared a home in Heaven for you, and that He will be with you in every sorrow and trial of life. "*. . . for he hath said, I will never leave thee, nor forsake thee.*" (Hebrews 13:5) "*God is our refuge and strength, a very present help in trouble.*" (Psalm 46:1)

❧ 4 ❧

LIVING IN THE WAVES

I LOVE THE WORDS OF THE HYMN WRITER H. G. Spafford:

> *"When sorrows like sea billows roll . . ."*

You may find yourself residing here for a while – living in the waves - living beneath the cloud of grief. *"For my days are consumed like smoke, and my bones are burned as an hearth. My heart is smitten, and withered like grass; so that I forget to eat my bread."* (Psalm 102:3-4)

You are doing fine . . . then you see a newborn at church. You are doing fine . . . then you drive past the hospital where you had your miscarriage procedure. You are doing fine . . . then you receive an invitation to a gender reveal party – The grief can certainly roll in and roll out like the tide. But there is a blessed promise from Heaven, in Isaiah 43:2 – *"When thou passest through the waters, I will be with thee; and through the rivers, they shall not overflow thee . . . For I am the LORD thy God . . ."* You are not alone. And this is not "the end."

Perhaps, like myself, you are writing:

> *I laugh and then wonder if it's wrong of me to*
> *laugh . . . I get worn out . . . I feel alone in the*
> *midst of the birthday party happenings, and in*
> *an instant, I WANT to be alone – to shut the*
> *door – to enjoy the quiet . . .*

You may have been fighting the battle with nausea, only a couple of weeks ago. Now you are "safe" to order country fried shrimp if you want. But the realization of that change can bring a flood of tears, right in the middle of Cracker Barrel! Sometimes you will not be able to bear standing within 50 feet of a newborn – it will break your heart to hear their cries. Other times, your arms will ache to hold the darling baby you see in the infant carrier at Walmart.

Maybe, like so many of us, you are plagued with all the "what ifs" and the "what might-have-beens." "Would he have been tall like his Daddy?" or "Did she have blue eyes like Mommy?" You may even be blaming yourself: "What if this happened because I lifted something too heavy? Or maybe my bath water, the other day, was too hot? Is this somehow my fault? I was not a good enough mother to keep the baby in my womb alive . . ." What the devil tries to feed you in your sorrow is not true – not a single word of it.

Psalm 94:19 declares, "*In the multitude of my thoughts within me thy comforts delight my soul.*"

There are certain things you will never know. Some questions will never have any answers. But even when those weighty thoughts are swirling through your mind, God's

Word can "put everything to rights." The pages of Scripture alone can help you reconcile every doubt and fear of your heart. After we said our farewells to Baby Joshua, I clung to ever so many of those pages. I cling to them again following the loss of Finlay. How I pray, you do the same!

FROM MY BLOG:

> *Ecclesiastes 3:4 tells us that there is "A time to weep . . . a time to mourn . . ." It is hard to explain all that God has brought us through during the past six weeks. In some ways, these weeks have been some of the longest in my life -The ups and downs in spirit; such waves of weeping and peace; feeling strong, and then feeling weak . . . But, as our pastor preached on New Year's morning, our Lord has left us His Comforter! (John 14:16) And how thankful we are that He did! Psalm 71:21 declares, "Thou shalt . . . comfort me on every side."*

> *And how faithfully He has done that! Through His Word, through the prayers of His people, through song . . . Psalm 147:3 "He healeth the broken in heart, and bindeth up their wounds."*

> *This month of January has been a month of learning about God's precious healing – a time like I have never known in any other stage of my life. So many afternoons I have sat on my bed with my Bible, a hymnal, a journal, and a ladies' devotional book, and felt God re-wrapping the bandages on my heart. Isaiah*

53:4 "Surely he hath borne our griefs, and carried our sorrows . . ." My Lord KNOWS, and He CARES . . . Through the alternating gloom and sunlight, I can pray the words of the beautiful hymn,

> *"When life's dark maze I tread,*
> *And griefs around me spread, Be Thou my Guide;*
> *Bid darkness turn to day, Wipe sorrow's tears away,*
> *Nor let me ever stray From Thee aside . . ."*

For some, it may take days; for others it may take months. But the fog does lift, My Friend. One day, you will look around you and suddenly realize that the sky is beautiful, that the grass is green, and that the dogwood in the front yard is blooming. I promise you. You will.

About a month after we lost our son, my husband walked through the door one evening with a Barnes & Noble membership and a *Downton Abbey* CD . . . It was a small and loving gesture to remind me that I was ALIVE. I treasure that memory.

You are not "yourself," all at once. It will take time before you are even physically and emotionally ready to leave the house. Perhaps your healthcare provider already made the obligatory phone call: "Are you eating? Are you sleeping at night? Are you having any thoughts of harming yourself?" During one of the difficult hours of his own life, King David wrote, "*I am weary with my groaning; all the night make I my bed to swim; I water my couch with my tears.*" (Ps. 6:6) If a week or more has passed since your miscarriage, you may find yourself ready for quiet distractions - hours spent writing down tearful thoughts in a journal, or painting, or creating a scrapbook. You NEED to take time for those things that can help you to HEAL.

But, perhaps, you already used too many tissues today. You still cannot even imagine looking through the ultrasound or the after-delivery photos of the baby you lost. You have read this section about "Living in the Waves," but, as far as you are concerned, this is no mere "water" surrounding you – it is bleak and overwhelming darkness. You want to sit in the shadows; you are not answering your phone calls; you have lost even the desire to eat. I want to leave you with the words of a precious hymn, Dear Sorrowing One – a hymn I have cried through more than once during my own dark days.

Turn Your Eyes Upon Jesus

"O soul are you weary and troubled?
No light in the darkness you see?
There's light for a look at the Savior,
And life more abundant and free:
Turn your eyes upon Jesus,
Look full in His wonderful face;
And the things of earth will grow strangely dim
In the light of His glory and grace."

❧ 5 ❧

THE OTHERS WHO NEED YOU

LIVING IN THE FOG AND THE WAVES – LIVING WITH GRIEF – can blind us to much of what is going on around us. The fact is, every little ache and pain seems more endurable during pregnancy – even the days of miserable nausea. There is REASON, there is PURPOSE, and there is the hope of something beautiful, through it all. But after the miscarriage, everything hurts . . . sometimes even the well-meaning words of family and friends.

Despite all that you are going through, there are others who need you, Dear One. Perhaps it is a husband. Perhaps it is other children. Perhaps it is a parent or a friend. There may be days that you have to ask the Lord to help you get out of bed in the morning, if only for them. In their love for you, they are grieving as well. They may not show it or express it in the same way. And no, they will not feel it the same as you do – they cannot. But they, too, are looking for healing. They are broken, seeing YOU broken. They lost a child, or a sibling, a cousin, or a grandchild. And in your pain and suffering, you have to ask the Lord to help you to see more than just yourself.

If even hugs hurt right now, you must be willing to express that. Marital intimacy can feel like something that will never return. You may not know about "trying again." At this moment in time, the very idea may make you quake with fear. As I look back over my journal, I find months of "What if I get pregnant again?" and "What if we have another miscarriage?" A traumatic tragedy is not "over" in a moment; sometimes, it is not "over" in a year. The only thing you can know – that you can truly cling to, for certain – is that when you ARE ready for your future, God will be there. He goes before us like the pillar of cloud in the daytime and the pillar of fire by night.

"And the LORD, he it is that doth go before thee; he will be with thee, he will not fail thee, neither forsake thee: fear not, neither be dismayed." (Deuteronomy 31:8)

No matter how much you are hurting, I plead with you not to give up on the man you love. You are in this sorrow together. Even when every part of your heart and body feels like it is crumbling to pieces, God can build your marriage relationship stronger than ever before. He can! Pray that way! Beg God that way!

For as long as I live, I will never forget the night Brandon came home to a depressed and tear-stained wife, sitting alone, in the hallway. He picked up the phone, asked his mom if she could watch our kids for us, and booked a room at our honeymoon spot. We needed to escape – whether intimacy was a part of the plan or not. The last time he and I had been alone for the night, we had been in a hospital room, weeping . . . *"My beloved spake, and said unto me, Rise up, my love, my fair one, and come away."* (Song of Solomon 2:10) This getaway was to be a memory for JOY! A memory for rebuilding. A memory for healing.

If you have other children at home, oh, how they need you too! Our first-grader, Brooklyn, has been coloring baby pictures of Joshua for over a year – she now adds Finlay to them as well. She goes down to the altar at church and prays for a "rainbow baby." She often expresses how much she misses having the siblings she lost. Our toddler Cheyenne marvels over every infant she sees. Children need hugs. They need a listening ear. They need proof that you understand their pain and that you love them immensely. God has left them with you during this time. You still have them to hold. Never take that for granted! They are a blessing and a joy.

But what if there are no other children? And what if you were told there will not be any more "trying again"? You see the pain in your husband's eyes, and you feel that you "let him down." The future you planned for yourselves is gone forever. No living babies . . . No pitter-patter of little feet. Such knowledge devastates and breaks the heart, but it does not mean you cannot LOVE! You may not be ready to consider words like "foster care" or "adoption" right now. But please know that there IS a future for you too! Even if God has said "no" to raising a child of your own, He still has a purpose and a plan for your life! YOU are SPECIAL to Him! "*For I am persuaded, that neither death, nor life . . . nor things present, nor things to come, Nor height, nor depth . . . shall be able to separate us from the love of God, which is in Christ Jesus our Lord.*" (Romans 6:38-39)

God loves you, Dear Lady! And nothing – NOTHING – can separate you from His love! Not even THIS.

"*A friend loveth at all times, and a brother is born for adversity.*" (Proverbs 17:17)

Friends, grandparents, cousins . . . They may not completely understand, but they know they want you "back." Even when it is hard, you have to let them know how you feel. Sometimes you may have to tell them "No." Not a "no" to all "girl nights" forever – just for now. You may have to explain that you need more time . . . that you need something quieter . . . or that you prefer a good cup of coffee in a bookstore to the hustle and bustle of the mall.

Perhaps others are begging to help. You are not sure you even want them to help. You may not be used to NEEDING anyone, but you do NEED them, more than you know. And sometimes THEY need to BE NEEDED by you! As much as they want to, they cannot take away the pain. However, they CAN help lighten your load. If they offer to do your dishes, I urge you to let them. If they want to bring you fast food from Chick-Fil-A, do not turn them down. Love is a precious and beautiful thing. Do not shut it out.

❧ 6 ❧

LOOKING AHEAD

"*. . . WEEPING MAY ENDURE FOR A NIGHT, BUT JOY COMETH IN the morning . . . Thou hast turned for me my mourning into dancing: thou hast put off my sackcloth, and girded me with gladness . . . O LORD my God, I will give thanks unto thee for ever.*" (Psalm 30:5, 11-12)

"*Behold, we count them happy which endure. Ye have heard of the patience of Job, and have seen the end of the Lord; that the Lord is very pitiful, and of tender mercy.*" (James 5:11)

In the months following our loss of Joshua, we saw God do such amazing, meaningful things. I want to share with you my reminiscing on that one-year anniversary of his delivery. I pray it will bring you HOPE – Hope that there is more in the life ahead of you than the painful tears of today . . . Hope that there IS a new tomorrow on your horizon, just as there was on mine . . . Just as I believe there will be for me again . . .

FROM MY BLOG:

Today, I pull out the comforting purple blanket

> *from the hospital, and I pray, thanking God for*
> *all He has brought us through. We talk at*
> *breakfast about what this last year in Heaven*
> *might have been like for Joshua. I look through*
> *the photos and the memory box. I remember*
> *the loving midwife, the nurses, our family, and*
> *our friends. I recall those who told us they were*
> *praying for us; those who wrote us messages*
> *and sent us cards; those who washed our dishes,*
> *and brought over taco salad or dinosaur*
> *chicken nuggets for our girls; those who reached*
> *out to us with precious remembrance gifts like*
> *wind chimes and necklaces . . . I praise God for*
> *His Word, and for the hymns of others who*
> *found the comfort of the Lord in great sorrow.*
> *I thank God for His loving care - that He "is*
> *good to all: and his tender mercies are over all*
> *his works." (Ps. 145:9) Today, I think back over*
> *this past year, and I say, "Look, with me, at*
> *what God alone could have done . . ."*

That year was one of the most incredible I have ever known. With my heart, I felt the grief and pain of sorrow, but I also knew the peace, the comfort, and the healing of my God. With my eyes, I saw the waves of Lake Erie, the mountains of West Virginia, and the rice paddies of Indonesia. I smelled the aromas of Asian spices and experienced the flavors of other parts of the world. I stood at the mouth of a volcano, rode on a motorbike, and watched two of my girls place their trust in Jesus Christ. As I clung to the Savior, I filled my mind with Bible verses, missions lessons, and research about countries I had never seen before. My hands planted wildflowers in a little memorial garden, built sandcastles with my girls, and packed and unpacked suitcases dozens of times. I had opportunities to sing God's praise, encourage women, and share with children, as we presented missions work in numerous churches across the Eastern United States. BLESSED in ways I could never have imagined, I saw my Lord at work everywhere around me. God gave me LIFE, and I began to appreciate the significance of that gift in a way I never had before.

How I pray, that in the days to come, you will look to see God's hand in your own life too, Dear One! There is no level of darkness that the light of God cannot touch. To Him, "*the night shineth as the day.*" (Psalm 139:12) Through every tear, He is right there beside you. Through every joy, His heart rejoices too.

Amid the smiles and the tears of life, may we pray with the Psalmist David, "*I will love thee, O LORD, my strength.*" (Psalm 18:1) I WILL . . . I will love You, secure in the knowledge that nothing can take away Your love for me. I will trust You, even when I do not understand. I will thank You, knowing that my baby is safe in the arms of Jesus. I will find hope in You – hope for this hour, this day, hope for the future ahead of me, and hope for all eternity. And even in the "*valley of the shadow of death,*" I will GLORIFY Your Name. "*Sing unto the LORD, bless his name; shew forth his salvation from day to day.*" (Psalm 96:2)

Ten years – a whole decade – before our first miscarriage, I penned a poem I entitled "*Unknown Trials.*" We don't know how much sorrow or joy will be in the steps that God has for our lives, but if we are His children, then we know that we can trust Him with our path. We are put here on this earth for just one purpose – to glorify our Father in Heaven. Even in our loss, we can bring glory to God – if we comfort others with "*the comfort wherewith we ourselves are comforted*" . . . if we point others to the cross . . .

if we let beauty rise from ashes . . . if in our sorrow, we offer
Him our praise.

Unknown Trials
August 2006

Half-way done with college,
My heart's now filled with dread.
I fear the tears and sorrows in
The life I have ahead.
Within my heart, I know
That God is ever near,
That He alone can take away
My every doubt and fear.
Again I give to Him
The future that is mine,
And pray, once more, "No, not my will,
But, O Lord, ever Thine."
Walking, hand in hand, Lord,
You'll never let me go.
In every trial of my life,
Your love for me You'll show.
Comfort, Lord, please give me,
And grace to meet those days,
And may I be a witness that
The lost might find their way.
Trials come, and trials pass,
But in them, might I shine.
I wish to be, in darkest times,
A candle, Lord, of Thine.

"*LET YOUR LIGHT SO SHINE BEFORE MEN, THAT THEY MAY SEE your good works, and glorify your Father which is in heaven.*" (Matthew 5:16)

"*Even every one that is called by my name: for I have created him for my glory, I have formed him; yea, I have made him.*" (Isaiah 43:7)

May you seek to shine, even in the darkness, Dear One. As you grieve the loss of your baby, may the Presence of God be real to you through every tear. May you take hold of HOPE – the true hope that is only found in our Savior, Jesus Christ. God Bless, My New Friend!

With All My Heart,
Kristen

❦

HYMN ACKNOWLEDGMENTS

- *Bow The Knee* – Words and Music By Chris Machen & Mike Harland – Arranged By Tom Fettke – Copyright 1997
- *All To Jesus I Surrender* – Judson W. Van DeVenter – 1896
- *Great is Thy Faithfulness* – Thomas O. Chisholm – 1923
- *Does Jesus Care?* – Frank E. Graeff – 1901
- *When Peace Like A River* – Horatio Gates Spafford – 1873
- *My Faith Looks Up To Thee* – Ray Palmer – 1830
- *Turn Your Eyes Upon Jesus* – Helen Howarth Lemmel - 1922

ABOUT THE AUTHOR

Kristen Kelley and her husband Brandon are missionaries to Southeast Asia. As a homeschooling mother of four little girls, Kristen thoroughly enjoys writing and teaching. She loves hats and flowers, historical dramas and musicals, buttery popcorn and the smell of pages in a printed book. Her devotionals for ladies come from a sincere desire to help others in their walk with the Lord.

Kristen blogs at:

DinnersintheOvenDevotional.blogspot.com

Write to Kristen at:
Peoples Baptist Church
3523 Spotswood Trail
Penn Laird, VA 22846

Made in the USA
Middletown, DE
31 March 2018